Letters *from* Deadman's Cay

Nina Berkhout

To the Nan Fam— Feb/03
Here's a little museum story!
Hope all is well, I miss
everyone very much!
Love Mina

NEWEST
PRESS

National Library of Canada Cataloguing in Publication Data
Berkhout, Nina, 1975-
Letters from Deadman's Cay / Nina Berkhout.
Poems.
ISBN 1-896300-65-0

I. Title.
PS8553.E688L47 2003   C811'.6   C2002-911454-3
PR9199.4.B48L47 2003

Editor for the Press: Don Kerr
Cover and interior photographs: Nina Berkhout
Darkroom work for cover and interior photographs: Hans Berkhout
Cover and interior design: Ruth Linka
Author photograph: Denise Berkhout

Some of the poems contained herein have appeared in a slightly
different form in *Grain, Lichen* and *Prairie Fire.*

The epigraph is an excerpt from "Lampfall" from *Collected Poems 1948-1984* by Derek Walcott.
Copyright © 1986 by Derek Walcott. Reprinted by permission of Farrar, Straus and Giroux, LLC.

  Canadian Patrimoine
Heritage canadien

NeWest Press acknowledges the support of the Canada Council for the Arts, the Alberta
Foundation for the Arts, and the Edmonton Arts Council for our publishing program. We also
acknowledge the financial support of the Government of Canada through the Book Publishing
Industry Development Program (BPIDP) for our publishing activities.

NeWest Press
201–8540–109 Street
Edmonton, Alberta T6G IE6
(780) 432-9427
www.newestpress.com

I   2   3   4   5   06   05   04   03

PRINTED   AND   BOUND   IN   CANADA

To the people of the island
who taught me so much

Contents

☙

But there's an old fish, a monster
Of primal fiction that drives barrelling
Undersea, too old to make a splash,
To which I'm hooked!
Through daydream, through nightmare trolling
Me so deep that no lights flash
There but the plankton's drifting, phosphorescent stars.

                            ∾ Derek Walcott, "Lampfall"

Within a Snowflake

Snow falls on the tired yellow city. I draw my curtains. Pack a new
prairie-gold bikini and swimsuit, glacier blue. The island is a spec of dust
in the atlas. Small as a sand particle within a snowflake, blown into the
atmosphere by wind.

Fleeing winter, following the birdpath south
toward the shade of white

palm trees. How many words
for sand?

✍

Two Miles Wide

Well I can't give details we've never actually *sent* anyone to this particular place, think of yourself as a missionary oh and I believe the pronunciation is Deadman's *kee* not *k-eh*. Two miles wide sixty miles long on the cusp of the Caribbean Sea and the Atlantic, how exotic! Wish the whole office could join you. Nothing on the internet? Of *course* it exists. Just not a major tourist destination anyway better run bon voyage remember to send

postcards.

✍

Arrival

Tincan plane skids across the landing strip like a pebble skipping water. A technicolour parrot shrieks WAKEUP! in my ear and suddenly

I am here.

On one of a thousand islands glinting like unstrung vertebrae across hundreds of miles of sea.

I duck out the aircraft door, eyes skimming landscape nervously. Why's the pilot laughing? Do I seem shocked by bush circling in on me, dirt road stretching grey before me leading to more bush? Do I appear astonished by the ringing sound all around me, surely cicadas, can't be silence never heard myself breathing back home, heart pounding loud as marching soldiers and how does the pilot float past so cool through air hotter than Hades, why do my arms redden at alarm-rapid rate, ankles and scalp crisping why didn't I think of hat and socks, skin melting faster than a candle in an oven, quick! someone scrape this sorry sight off the tarmac

dump your shade bucket onto me.

～

Paper Umbrellas for Tropical Drinks

No dad, can't hear you just my own voice bouncing back at me wrapping
round my headache will the echo ever
disappear?

Everyone stares when I pass, sis, my house is along the highway no I
haven't seen ocean yet just bush and too much sky bleeding blue, no not
like prairie vastness it's an open wound above me can't hide anywhere,
dialogue so thick don't understand a thing have to keep asking them to
repeat 'til yesterday the preacher finally said *you deaf, chile?*

So. Hot. Here. Mom.
I've landed in the middle of noplace, please send more
Muskol. Gravol too.

What, dear? Can't hear you're right bad echo, sure we'll pop supplies in
the mail shouldn't take more than a few days your sister sent Toblerone, a
beach towel and paper umbrellas for tropical drinks do you think
the chocolate
will melt?

☞

Blue Hole

Fingernails curl like seashells on this island. The bonefisherman casts
my aging reflection into a blue hole beneath salt waves. Nothing has
surfaced. No letter, no photo, no cracked coral voice, just

a serpent's brittle jaw grinning along the shoreline
of the world's deepest ocean hole, shaped
like a hawksbill turtle.

I am the lead-heavy counterfeit coin.
Toss my burning body like a discus away from the sun.

Viola

Chile, you seen dat white lady livin next door? Old Viola Turnquest asks her
granddaughter and from then on she follows me with her knuckles.
I'm creeping past her cornfield hoping she won't hear me but always she
comes hissing out of the bush frightening me to death with her cutlass and
her milky eyes, questioning me, the old haggard sphinx, each time I try to
pass. Her hands are more worn than a redwood forest. I think of legends,
of Isoldt of the White Hands and I secretly call her Viola of the Black
Hands, Viola of the Black Roosters haunting me during my sojourn here.
Yes, Viola has three black roosters obeying her every command, her
Cerberus, her underworld hundred-eyed dog because Viola can't see me
she's blind.

❧

Museum

I am to set up a museum. I have an empty building, painted pink by Dutch Boy. Each day, I visit the island's settlements to collect artifacts and stories. When I knock on doors the islanders say *why, lady? We got no photographs of ourself and de ole stuff, we trew in da dump.* Museum is my religion but God is the religion of Deadman's Cay.

MUSEUM:
an almost perfect palindrome

I once worked in a place where cherrywood chairs were worth thousands and paperweights pressed papers of kings and queens. Violins and harpsichords were auctioned off at millions of dollars, tapestries were woven with gold thread.

Here, I draw music from the island dump. Gin bottles and spoons, rusty saws, the skin of a goat. Straw mats are $5 each and glassworks are free from the sea.

In the end it is all the same. A mosaic dome or a carpet of shells, the royal chair or the sisal chair, crimson tapestry or straw mat, Lalique vase or ocean glass.

See that dockmaster forever staring out to sea? I'd like to encase Him.

☞

Skin of a Fish

Moving forward through leagues of water and white sand I think of snowdrifts. What pattern do I tread upon, what mandala do the waves continually sketch and erase? And where on earth *is* everyone? But wait— here is a tropical fish at my feet. Dying, its skin changing colour like a mood ring.

The Fisherman's Wife

She calls when her husband is out to sea. We have a country in common.
"Why here?" I ask. "To rebel against strict parents, a private school
upbringing and a law degree from Montreal," she replies. "I told my girl-
friends *Allons aux Bahamas cet hiver, les filles!* but love fell over me,
didn't count on that so the girls flew back to Canada that winter without
me. You should do the same, plenty of fish here for you to choose from!"
she says. This fisherman's wife left a vast cold continent behind for a
scorching island the size of St. Joseph's Oratory. Her little ones run
around barefoot, unaffected by sandspurs or stinging ants. Toddlers that
have the ocean in their eyes, who already understand the sea better than
I ever will. She has a few strands of grey hair, which she dyes black since
there is only black hair dye to be had on the island. It suits her with her
gold skin, green eyes. The women despise her. She is different she is
liberal she does not attend church and most importantly she does not have
a Big Ass. A sylph floating above the bush the heat and all other general
unpleasantness the island sometimes brings, the fisherman's wife is the
sea nymph of Deadman's Cay. And because she is in love with her
fisherman there is bitterness and a feeling of malaise from the women here
who prey on lovers like sea vamps hunting collarbones.

〰

Bat Moths

Are they big black butterflies? NO dey be called bat moths watch out, dey stink and swoop down and when dem tings collide wit you dey'll stain your clothes black in your case dey'll stain your skin black too we're lucky we don't have to worry none bout dat.

Driving

Some nights, when her husband is out to sea, the fisherman's wife puts on a bright batik wrap and fuchsia lipstick. There is nowhere to go. "Let's get dressed up and pretend there's somewhere to go!" she says. We drive up and down the sole road that crosses the island. We stop at *Coco's*. I wait in the car while the fisherman's wife runs inside the bar for two Kaliks, the Bahamian beer named for the sound of cowbells, *kalik, kalik, kalik.* We drive and gossip like schoolgirls. She cranks up her stereo and I feel young again. On nights without moonlight we pull over and catch bush crabs scuttling across the road. She throws them in the trunk of her car until she can lock them into a cage at home where she will fatten them up with johnnycake for a week before boiling them. We stop at *Da Danz* for a second Kalik and we drive, stop and lie on the hood of the car watching stars heavy and low like wet sand, while sandflies inflict constellations of their own across our skin. We pull over at blue holes and I sit on the edge while she skinny dips. "See, marry someone here and we could do this all the time wouldn't that be fun you'd be the envy of your friends freezing their buns off back home you'd be living in paradise!"
If.
There is love.
Yes.

Paradise.

These nights with the fisherman's wife I'm happy, in control of the primeval island. When the men are out to sea I have a friend but when they return I'm alone again on this rock.

☙

Baubles in Trees

Giant baubles hang from the trees. When there is a breeze they bob up and
down like colourful jester's crowns. Plastic dolls, styrofoam buoys,
frisbees, empty bleach bottles. All things washed ashore are good omens
from the Other Worlds. But don't confuse baubles with glass bottles
hanging from fruit trees. The bottles containing dark liquids and darker
spells are Obeah. Take one of these fruit and *you dead, bulla*. Don't ever
say the O-word out loud. If anyone finds you practicing, you'll go straight
to Her Majesty's Prison. I met a man who stayed in his house seven years
under an O-curse. He owed the O-practitioner money, never paid up and
was cursed into a zombie state until the O-practitioner died. The very day
of the funeral, the cursed man miraculously rose from his bed, kissed his
wife on the cheek, opened the door and stepped into the Bahamian sun for
the first time in seven years. As if nothing had happened. Now he owns
Da Danz nightclub where he dances all night long. He uses a hand carved
cane to hook around the necks of hooligans who misbehave, tossing them
out of his club with a smack on the head. This ex-cursed man has the
deepest voice I've ever heard. A voice that speaks in urns.

❧

The Preamble I Forgot to Mention

Before I left Canada for the island, I had a lover. Let me rephrase that. I left Canada and came to the island, in part because I had a lover. When a "you" is addressed in these passages I am talking to the lover, the "you"* is him and I have not bothered to name him he is neither here nor there, though sometimes I miss him and this will come out in what I have written. At times, I imagine him here with me. We were the Dogs of War together, he and I, for two long years. We fought and loved like Alsatians. I don't know what's become of him because he walked away from me when I said, "I'm going to a small island to be rid of you." He sucked his teeth and glared at the pavement and replied, "Thank God now get out of my sight."

*please refer to the following poem

Slow Ascent

I imagine you here. You climb ahead on rocks black and slick as sealskin. I slip behind, hearing only the crunch of bare feet crushing shells. You move on as I kneel down, trying to find a snail still living. In a warm hollow of water I pull one from its rock—with a faint *schllluck* sound, the creature sighs. Marching forward, impatient, you swing your head back toward me: "Bleeding teeth. They call those *bleeding teeth!*" and, vague as seafoam, you vanish up the cliff while I, still kneeling, poke at the pink-red flesh, eye the tiny meaty thing throbbing inside its shell before receding into empty space.

☙

Dutch Boy

He helped paint the inside of my museum, he'll paint whatever needs painting on the island and Dutch Boy is the brand he uses, hence the nickname. He must be nearing forty though it's hard to tell what's behind all that hair. Looks as though he just emerged from Hamilton's Cave after a long hibernation. He never wears shoes and I admire this. He's so quiet that at first I wondered if he was mute. I tried speaking with him but he just smiled down at me from his ladder then looked up again, continued painting neat white
brush strokes delicate
like sea urchin spines.

When he's not out to sea, Dutch Boy lies on top of the old sloop sailboat marooned beneath a cork tree. He folds his arms in a diamond behind his head and stares at the clear blue sky. I want to know what he's thinking. Is he willing a cloud to appear? This will never happen. More likely he's telling the sky to stay and not change, stay and not change. The fisherman's wife assures me that Dutch Boy is a philosopher. Maybe the philosopher thinks nothing at all and it is this possibility which angers me the most, which I uselessly try to grasp like a slippery wahoo. Dutch Boy lying on a boat beneath the cork tree staring at the sky for a lifetime, with no desire to ever leave the island. *What else is there, Fools?* he thinks to himself. The island's philosopher is laughing at all of us and especially at the pasty city girl. Dutch Boy there's much more than this, I would respond, but if asked, *what's more?* I couldn't answer.

Hurricane

There are dead fish in the trees, some slapped comically atop the buoys and dolls. A family of lizards living in my house died from fright. The wind has left me with a horrible earache. It burnt the life from plants and trees and flowers and those still living have turned a sickly yellow. "Our Bahamian sky and sun are most beautiful after a hurricane!" the fisherman's wife tells me. "These storms cleanse the sky, rendering it more blindingly blue than ever." Intolerable. Inhuman island sky and sun, cutting my vision like a mote. Hurricane means flooding means swamp water means:

sandflies breeding sandflies breeding sandflies breeding sandflies breeding
sandflies breeding sandflies breeding sandflies breeding sandflies breeding
sandflies breeding sandflies breeding sandflies breeding sandflies breeding
sandflies breeding sandflies breeding sandflies breeding sandflies breeding
sandflies breeding sandflies breeding sandflies breeding sandflies breeding
sandflies breeding sandflies breeding sandflies breeding sandflies breeding
sandflies breeding sandflies breeding sandflies breeding sandflies breeding
sandflies breeding sandflies breeding sandflies breeding sandflies breeding
sandflies breeding sandflies breeding sandflies breeding sandflies breeding
sandflies breeding sandflies breeding sandflies breeding sandflies breeding
sandflies breeding sandflies breeding sandflies breeding sandflies breeding
sandflies breeding sandflies breeding sandflies breeding sandflies breeding

Museum Display Panel #1: BUSH MEDICINE

Prior to the 1950s, there was no health care delivery system for The Bahamas family islands. The people of the out-islands resorted to curing themselves with the natural resources available. Often, they learned of healing plants by trial and error, and through watching what the animals ate. A popular saying amongst Bahamians is, *Whatever the critter done eat, in particular goats and sheep, you can eat.* Today, health care is accessible throughout the country, yet Bahamians continue their tradition of using native flora medicinally, a practice known as *Bush Medicine*, tracing back over 200 years ago, to when slaves came to The Bahamas from West Africa.

A number of bushes are said to have medicinal value and can be used to cure a variety of ailments from asthma and the common cold, to boosting energy and producing fertility in women. Some of the bushes are thought to have the qualities of an aphrodisiac, and bear intriguing names such as

Life Leaf
Sailor's Flowers
Seven-Man Strength

Five Fingers
Love Vine
Strong Back

and Touch Me Not.

Hummingbirds

One of the only bird species residing on the island, they appear then disappear from the corner of my left eye. They move too quickly, it's unnatural and makes me nervous that one day their tiny hearts will stop. Hummingbirds would rain down from all the hibiscus blossoms in Deadman's Cay, and from the Jesus Christ tree near the Clarence Town Church, which blooms blood red at Easter.

❧

Alma

Her mind no longer bothers correcting the upside-down, inverted image of
the island as it passes through the eye's pinhole. Alma Darville knows to
forget. She walks the old dirt road outliving us all, Alma and her silent,
sand-coloured potcake dog leashed on a strand of Christmas lights. Alma
stands near the children. Tamarind spinning tops skip on concrete like
young hearts unravelling at her feet but never mind . . . Alma with an ice
cream cone. *How old I is?* She asks at sunrise. Older than the turquoise of
your Bahamian sky and sea, Alma. Knotted fingers twisting grey
cornbraids, up and down the old dirt road, requesting a white page from
the grocer, a sheet a day to grasp blank. Unwritten. Another reason I know
you savvy, Alma.

✍

Beneath my Window

All night long my stomach swells with plated bodies of seahorses. Beneath my window, a flamingo preens himself grey with the morning sickness of a waning moon. Is it the rake and scrape of a beak in rich red soil or the shadow of wings brushed with faint constellations?

Nobody remembers.

The bird collects bones from banana holes and drops them at my feet.

❧

Sailing

The fisherman's wife and her fisherman pick me up one Saturday to take me for a boat ride. Dutch Boy comes along and never says a word. Yesterday I saw him with a wild boar slung over his shoulder, walking down the Queen's Highway. The fisherman and his wife are Love. They do not Sweetheart on each other like the other men and women, they do not fool around, they know what they have is Good. They take me to an uninhabited, lone isle, I watch them from the shore they are far far far in turquoise holding onto one another.　　　Pang. Me, I'm sweethearting my own shadow. Dutch boy comes along and never says a word. Someone slips away from me, something calls me home.

✿

Cartwright's Gospel Chapel Cemetery

This week the Brethren dig a grave. This week I struggle to write the museum brochure on a carnival display and fugitive costumes that last the length of a midnight parade. Sunrise hits the tombs, casting bright lozenges into the gallery (technicolour light if a grave dons plastic flowers, watery light if there be no recently buried). Two in the hole digging, a dozen others congregated around their heads, discussing politics and sweethearting. Shirtless rum drinkers shaded by mangroves shout from high in the branches: *when you havin such a good time laughin, you gonna get sadness*, almost in unison, almost scolding the Dead One. What to say of ravens on stilts lunging toward street revelers or the transience of fringed, craypaper cloaks? Paraders torching costumes at dawn, my display table a pyre. Sunset illuminates the limestone beds next door. The Brethren pack up their belongings and one man mutters, as he passes near my window, *woulda been easier to burn her.*

∞

JUNKANOO Display Panel: Rough Draft

Junkanoo *is a pan-Caribbean festival which began in the Bahamas during the pre-Emancipation Era, when slaves were granted a special holiday at Christmas time. Slaves left their plantation site to visit relatives, and celebrated their holiday with dance and music. Although there are numerous theories concerning the origins of Junkanoo, it is certain that the Bahamian Festival has distinct African traits, and it is commonly believed that Junkanoo was derived from African masked rituals. After the Emancipation Act of 1834, Junkanoo celebrations continued each year in The Bahamas, until the event established itself as a national festival.*

Junkanoo is celebrated both on Boxing Day and on New Year's Day, in the early hours of the morning, winding up after sunrise. At early Junkanoo parades, revelers wore "scrap" costumes made from strips of cloth, bright bits of material, cardboard, and sponge. Whistles, goatskin drums, horns, and cowbells created the trademark sound, while individuals in colourful crepe-paper attire paraded through streets in a slow, dancing march known as "rushing."

As we Bathe

You are wrong. Absence does not vanish with time, but rests in the white amnesia of sand, or the curved and cured baleen arc drying in the sun. Something is always licking its paws, someone frames the longings of the lepidopterist collecting sable moths, and as we bathe absinthe-green wreaths of plankton mourn around our wrists so you are wrong. The ocean's tiered fugue never tires of reminding.

✍

Christmas

The sweaty moon waxes and wanes up and down rather
than side to side.

It's Christmas and I'm reading *Kamouraska*, snow and cold in the heart of
Quebec, trying to find winter in this tropical landscape where I emit an
acrid body odor I can't seem to wash from myself. Books I carried here:
Wuthering Heights, Women in Love. Stupid pale girl.

Christmas Eve, I dream I'm pursued by giant icicles. Drums and chanting
and voices in trees. I look through my photo album to mountains and my
family. Waterfalls trickling, I smell pine and see breath clouds.

All is still tonight, even
roosters are mute Christmas eve.

Walking along the beach Christmas day I find a cruise ship bottle
containing a business card. Church service. Hold a neighbour's hand and
pray. A preying mantis on my windowsill tonight. The fisherman's wife
tells me this is a good omen. Glowing green it has largesadeyes and legs
like a ballerina is it me? No, not my legs, it stares me straight down
doesn't move.

☙

Paradise Island

Treasure seekers with metal detectors are led to the macaw who hides colour deep in a tree trunk. Fools from ships comb our island's deserted beaches, gathering truckloads of shells for Miami resorts, sailing away the same day they arrive. On stifling turquoise nights, shells are strewn on Florida sand by hotel staff (guests, bloated, burnt dumb, bob up and down in the water). What tarnished amulet, what undertow of civilizations has this bird swallowed?

✍

Mister and Missus Stubbs

In the settlement of Burnt Ground, where houses have no windows or
doors, everybody happy to be livin another day God willin. Mister Stubbs
gives me shellwork for the museum. Missus Stubbs, tiny and crinkled like
a wrinkle-lipped bat, points to me from her armchair and says, "next time
you come I make you cake!" I did not hear correctly I'm busy watching
mice burrowing beneath her bandaged foot. She repeats herself, "next
time you come I make you cage! A cage, snowbird. A golden cage I put
you inside and I keep you." Looking up at me, bright licorice eyes, after a
long pause   "I love you. Don't know why but I love
you."   Ah, me.

And I'll build *you* a feathered barge
with sweepings from my moulting cage floor.

෴

Cataloguing Bones

Sandflies silence the dunes, buoys mute the water. I hear but a faint
wheezing as I braid solitude into baskets for fish heads and empty shells.
Remembering you once each day, like the pineapple plant that bears a
single fruit then dies. Sun strikes silver top palm and pink conch, blinding
me. Sandpiper braille is washed to sea. I'm collecting for you, on this
beach, bleached skeletons of small sea creatures pressed between rocks
like fossilized lovers.

Samuel Simms

Near the settlement of Dunmore, half a mile past the hand-painted sign:

```
SAMMY'S STRAW WORKS ENTERPRISE
         Dunmore Bahamas
```

turn left take the path through the corn field to the clearing and in the
distance see him sitting on his crimson velvet couch in the open field,
shaded by the Lignum Vitae. Meet Samuel Simms Master Weaver. (In the
ESSO baseball cap and parrot-patterned shirt. The only one in the field
besides the tree.) Whistling hymns, Samuel invents new patterns, a gospel
of baskets and fanners and trays spread around him. Unaffected by the
scorching heat and the blistering sun. Because IT Has Always Been So.
Suffering bring Revelation Samuel Simms know this. Golden plait
clippings mark his Bible, especially in The Book of Psalms: three pearl,
peas n' rice, eleven string, fishscale. Samuel rests only on Sundays. He's
named his latest design Jacob's Ladder, where black stands are
miraculously interwoven with golden palm. Just last night, he accidentally
discovered how to blacken the palm straws, when he absentmindedly held
his bible marker too close to the lantern, while reading The Twenty-Third
Psalm. Above the flickering flame the marker shone ebony Samuel Simms
knew he'd been granted a Sign from Above.

☙

Gossip

Now here's a story an old lady lit herself and her house on fire last week everybody talkin bout dat nasty woman. She been pure evil and black as tar herself don't know how she could see, bein so black and imagine the nerve, never lettin blacks near her house, trowin stones at us and if anyone be deliverin money to her, she be makin us trow dat money on the ground an she be pourin salt on it before pickin it up. All dat blackness advancin down de road good ting we got rid of her but let's go to de funeral gal, I got a new hairpiece to wear.

Lizards

Why do they keep getting trapped in my windows between the screens and panes of glass why dry up and die still in motion why not go do that in distant Pompeii not in front of me tiny gravemarkers tiny reminders that are my bookmarks look how scaly I have become.

❧

Orlando Knowles

Sitting in a rocking chair plaiting silvertop palm, surrounded by straw, this old man braids stories more colourful than stained glass. Orlando Knowles is eighty-nine but he can't remember that. Nor does he recall the corn grits and steamed mutton his wife prepared for him at dinner. He breaks into song and begins reciting from his Royal Readers collection, word for word verses memorized in childhood. A boy skating on a winter canal in a dark forest, pursued by a pack of wolves. "Ain't never seen snow wolves ice skates but I lived 'em inside here." Taps his heart. "Have I told you dat wolf and skates story yet?" I replay his voice for him on the tape recorder, he gives me a proud schoolboy grin. Hugs me when I leave. "You sigh like Thomas Hardy," he says.

❦

This is the Place for the Almost Dead

"Nothing ages here," the fisherman's wife tells me. Her husband's trip to
sea has been unusually long and she's suffering from Melancholia.
Tonight we're not laughing we drive without music. "The old people have
always been old and the young ones always leave so nothing ages here but
watch out when you go home you'll see that Time has passed." She lights
her cigarette, exhales. "See how the elders sit in their houses, quietly
weaving straw? Seems like they're waiting for something, doesn't it?
When you go on your settlement visits you're probably the first visitor
they've had in years. *Who dat knockin is it Time?* they wonder before
opening the door. They're secretly hoping you're the reaper come
knocking." She takes a sip of her Kalik. "Unlike you and me, they have
The Faith. Me, I know this is as close to Paradise as I'll ever get. For them
it's just a passage to the final resting place. This is the place for the
Almost Dead. They'll sail away one day and then maybe this island will
sink. They want to attain something like that Dilmun haven
Gilgamesh tried to reach. Or King Arthur's Avalon. Guess nobody taught
these people that Utopia means Noplace in Greek." The car lurches to a
hault and the fisherman's wife swings the door open to catch a crab,
adding, "By the way Dutch Boy cut his hair for you and bought a pair of
shoes."

❧

Alexander's Dark Band

I find myself in a labyrinth more complicated than brain coral, night is
falling I'm with others who make their way out as the tide begins to rise
and flood the maze. I'm busy groping for sea glass, on my hands and
knees in the dark. I can't get enough sea glass and won't leave the maze
until I've collected all the shards in Deadman's Cay. The others leave me
there to drown and I awake feeling like the dead black space between two
rainbows (all rainbows come in pairs). That dreaded space scientists call
Alexander's Dark Band.

ॐ

Serenades in the Grass

On the occasion of The Green Flash, Dutch Boy delivers a bouquet of wild
orchids wrapped in orange vine.

"Did you see the sunset's green flash?" he asks.

I lie and respond, "of course."

"They're rare, most foreigners can't see them," he continues, and this is
the most I've heard Dutch Boy speak in five months. I'd like to invite him
inside but I resist. My longing is still spread like a red shroud over the
skull of an old Alsatian. Me, I'm still cataloguing bones. With his new
haircut now I see Eyes that are lapis lazuli blue like the hair of Egyptian
deities. Simultaneously, we look down at his brown loafers.

I say, "Dutch Boy doesn't the world sound loud in shoes?"

He replies, "and heavy like plantation ruins."

Walking back into the night, his footprints leave serenades in the grass.
All at once I hear an albumen pulse beating like the soft heart of a jellyfish
but is this my pulse or his?

∞

Why, When the Sun Sets Green

After years of watching sunsets flashing blue then green then vanishing,
eyelids barnacled, we ask ourselves, *why?* Like starfish, we've slowly
picked our way over the bottom of the sea, smelling out our choices until
suddenly, Time is up. *So why hold on?* For an agonizingly pure and white
geometry of crumpled pieces of paper suctioned to the edge of my desk,
day and night like pale anemones. And for the soldier crab pacing on top
of Chimney Rock, gone madder than old Ajax, for the soldier crab pincing
his *own* claws off before *he'd* abandon his last shell to the surge (the
osprey dropped him here, he knows he's going to die). Simple things,
really. Red bunches of bottlebrush resembling rooster tails, and for the
black rooster outside my window whose cry is fitted with a sharp metal
spur – for the one who offered to take me into the darkness of my own ear,
I cling to shore and watch sunsets flashing

green.

Along the Backbone of my Skin

Seagulls cleave the morning air, screeching. "Come on, our seagulls laugh here, we call them May Laughenders they cackle so much, don't be so moody," the fisherman's wife says to me. "Have some gin and coconut water, you'll feel better it'll help get rid of that wintry sleigh driving you home."

The fisherman's wife can't understand that the grains of sand running along the backbone of my skin cause pain.

Her long eyelashes are bladed weapons tonight.

❧

21-Gun Salute

Bulla you tellin me you been tryin to cure dat limpness wit conch? Mon
dat be an aphrodisiac for woman ain't gonna cure what you got no way, go
see Uncle Drake he'll set you straight wit a bottle of 21-Gun Salute, dat
black nigger charge way way for dem bottles he know dey good, drink dat
bulla an one hour later you be harder an more erect dan dem plantation
pillars we still got standin in da bush, hell I ain't got no idea what Uncle
Drake put in dat drink, likely tree roots an such but Ole Clifton down da
road, he say Uncle Drake pay Dutch Boy to get dem wild boar hearts,
maybe it be dat wild boar heart givin us new life down below.

❧

Skin of a Goat

Sand stretched taut around the edge of the island like the skin of the goombay drum. Today, I come across a dead calf washed upon the shore. Water licks its legs and bends its neck backward into an arabesque. Tide is rising and still I can't bring myself to move the body. The fur and sand are the same glistening browns, the same pulse and were you here I'm certain you'd run home for your brushes and easel, to paint a mirage with a plaque reading, *find the sand calf.*

&

Meanwhile, In My Museum I Write

THE GOATSKIN DRUM

Historically, secular music in The Bahamas is called Goombay music, the word "goombay" emerging from the *goom-bay* beat of the goatskin drum. The drum, *"a pounding extension of the heartbeat,"* is an integral part of Bahamian secular music, which relies on this type of drum to create its rhythmic base. Whereas in the past, goatskins were stretched over lard kegs, cheese boxes, nail kegs, and salt beef barrels, today, oil barrels are often used to create a powerful pulsing beat.

To make a drum, the goatskin is first shaven clean and pulled tight over a fire. Once both ends of the barrel are cut open, the skin of the goat is pulled tightly across and fastened over one of the openings. If the drum is played for long periods of time, the drummer can rest a small flame inside the instrument
to keep the skin taut.

Resurrection

You cursed the lunatic moon limping across the sky, fickle stars winking
secrets over and over again, the ocean whose trickeries you grew to
despise. But there is an ending where we die like sponges cut from the
ocean floor and cast upon the rocks, when passers-by will hold their breath
for the stench of our flesh, decomposing under the sun.

Do you regret the stars now?

Somebody takes pity, he wades knee deep in the water and slaps our
remains onto a wooden plank: hear the *thwack, thwack, thwack* of
cleansing, an old man strings us together with his needle carved from the
heart of a white torch tree. He hangs us to dry on his clothesline. The sun
has no choice but to set through our pores hollowed
golden brown

the living scour their flesh with our bodies.

Lost

Alma be lost! cries Missus Stubbs, Alma's sister. *Why didna I put her in cage, she wouldna be lost then!* she weeps. Alma was last seen yesterday morning near the salt ponds. Balanced on an abandoned sloop boat boom, dipping her feet in the murky water, as witnessed by islanders who walked past and waved according to custom. She wore a pale purple bathrobe pulled above the knees and Miss Faye Morris noted that, from the highway, her new Jacob's Ladder straw visor (a gift from Samuel Simms), flecked gold gills through her silver curls.

☙

Where our Rakes Can't Reach her No More

We find Alma's potcake resting in the mangroves, an extension cord slack around its neck. It whimpers then growls as Dutch Boy approaches to untie it from the tree. I join the fishermen surrounding the ponds. Dutch Boy hands me a rake with a long, crooked handle that slithers like an eel through the water.

The mutt's eyes remain fixed on a torn bit of paper, a

floating

        frangipani

        petal

        small enough to be

                missed.

Alma drifts far beneath the withered skin of the pond, where our long-toothed prongs can't reach her no more. *The salt'll preserve her soul did she ever tell you her name meant soul* Dutch Boy says, walking away with his head bent low.

☙

The Grotesque

The dog wanders along the Queen's Highway dragging the extension cord
in its mouth, howling every night until old Viola curses it to silence. From
my bedroom window, I catch her sticking fireflies on her toes, to spot
snakes on the path late at night. There's been no trace of the mutt for a
week. Ignoring all accusations, Viola mumbles to her birds . . . *Dat woman*
be tryin to determin future events by dippin her feet in dem ponds, lookin
for patterns, dat be why she drown.

This morning, trekking through the bush toward the pools, The Grotesque
slaps my nostrils like a pack of voodoo lilies. I run away before seeing
what the salt pond disgorged.

☞

Cuckoo Soup

"What'd you do to Dutch Boy, feed him cuckoo soup?" the fisherman's wife asks me. "What's cuckoo soup?" I cringe as I plunge my feet into a bucket of ice. I've had my first encounter with stinging ants, playing in the yard with her children. "Obeah," she whispers, placing a basket of peas on the table and calling to the little ones to bring me garden aloe. "In this case, love magic for whoever eats the soup. Usually ends badly. Anyway, since I've known him, Dutch Boy just lies on that damned boat, *thinking*, but now he's up and building a boat of his own." Her barefoot daughter runs inside with the leaves, glances at my swollen feet, runs away giggling as my ankles swell into sea cucumbers. Peeling the aloe, the fisherman's wife catches my flushed expression and notes in singsong, pointing to my legs, "Chile, dis be da least of your worry worry here gal!"

❧

Boat Building

Dutch Boy: *I'll name her Snowbird.*

Museum Text: Living in an Archipelago, Bahamians have relied on boats as a means of transportation, for centuries. In the early years of boat building, before electricity and power were available, the work was done entirely by hand. Even today, many designs used by boat builders resemble the designs their forefathers employed over two hundred years ago. Most boats are still built manually with hand tools such as the chisel, jackplane, saw, maul and nail set, and axe.

Dutch Boy: *See if she'll sail me to Canada then back.*

Museum Text: When possible, woods native to The Bahamas are employed to make the boats. The horse-flesh, madeira, wild tamarind, lignum vitae, dog wood and bull wood are all Bahamian hard woods which can serve as boat frames. Pine fir, cyprus or white cedar are the preferred woods for boat planking.

Dutch Boy: *For an amulet, I'll paint a white bird next to her name. Winter bird goin back an forth so long as I can get home again gotta be able to come back home.*

Museum Text: In relation to boats, sailing, and nostalgia for their homeland, a favorite Bahamian tune is the Calypso version of *Sloop John B.*

෴

Obeah Tip

If you happen to be walkin home round midnight an you arrive at a crossroad, you be wise to remove your shirt, turn it inside out an put it on again. Spit tree times East, tree times West; proceed along your way. Den, gal, you be reachin home protected from molestation by restless spirits roamin wild at night.

Oh, an if you hear a chile whistlin' in your house, beware for dat mean Calamity be comin.

☙

Soup and Tooth in a Bottle

The week I stay home, bloated with parasites, Dutch Boy comes knocking.
"Got some soup for you," he says, "and a bottle for your windowsill. From
the underbelly of a nurse shark." Something rattles inside the square,
seaweed-tinted bottle as he passes it to me. I tilt it upside down and a
sharp, white tooth falls out. "A Key Gin bottle. I hear you got Dutch blood
in you. These bottles come from over there, this one's older than you n'
me together." The sun catches the bottle's surface scratches, tossing a net
of light over the red seastar lying next to it. When I sip the hot soup, still
staring at the bottle, old Viola's roosters begin crowing like demented
town criers.

✍

Memories are Pebbles in Sandals

The blood oranges I press into a ruby juice drink are bitter on my lips like the sun's final rays. I wander across the island playground, where memories are pebbles in sandals.

(The sun snuck something away. I am forgetting you.)

So why not leave our smiles in the Dead Stone Room? Sweep them into a powder horn, preserve the ones we love. Let's grind down alabaster veins, filter them into snuff bottles, silly little colourful remnants of the parade.

Entomb pumiced hearts, cold frills and spines grating
raw
calloused memory.

(Conservators call it an *inherent vice*: the acidity in wood allows paper to eat away at itself. Your words and mine licked from letters until our messages shed their skin, disappearing like the dragonfly.)

☙

Horned Hog Turtle

The museum is the new gathering place for islanders. The men have
deserted the graveyard next door to sit on my front porch. Mister Stubbs
brings in a colossal sculpture for the entranceway. The *horned hog turtle*
comprises the horns of a goat, cemented to the skull of a hawskbill turtle,
with wild boar tusks fastened to each corner of the skeleton's grinning
mouth. The sculpture is coated in bleeding teeth, cowries, snail and tiger
shells. "Spent many a boyhood hour collectin shells from the marsh and
beach, cleanin 'em one by one, pastin em individuly onto my statues," he
says, shaking his head in wonder, running a hand along his creation to
wipe off a layer of dust.

✎

First Sail

Returning from the museum this evening, I find a note wedged in my
doorframe: Join me tomorrow at dawn for first sail.
But I toss and turn, old Viola's roosters crow all night long, ululating until
just before sunrise, when I finally fall asleep . . .
It's late morning by the time I awake and run to the shore.
The dock is empty.

May Laughenders bicker above me, rising and falling
in unison with the waves.

I squint toward the horizon and see one pale wing suspended above the
ocean: far off in the distance, Dutch Boy is sailing away on the Snowbird.

෴

Bye and Bye

Rupert Buckley bringing in artifacts for the "Music and Celebrations" display: guitar, harmonica, accordion, conch horn. Sing for me let me record you, I plead. *Sure ting, Gal.* Rupert, castaway musician in continuous elation, accompanying a barge of angels:

Bye and Bye

Said when the morning comes
all the saints of God are gatherin' on
we gonna tell, say how we overcome
we done understand it better bye and bye

said but one of those bright mornings, bright and soon
not a cricket not a spirit, Lord done shout me on
when I reaching Heaven, I'll understand it now
I done understand it better bye and bye

Children, it's bye and bye
when the morning comes
and all the saints of God are gatherin' on
we gonna tell Jesus how we overcome
Lord we'll understand it better bye and bye

A for this ark, he was a wonderful boat
built him on the land, she get water, get to float
B now for the beast at the ending of the wood
now we understand it better bye and bye

Children, it's bye and bye
when the morning comes
and all the saints of God are gatherin' on
we gonna tell Jesus how we overcome
Lord we'll understand it better bye and bye . . .

෴

Display Panel: RAKE 'N SCRAPE MUSIC

Rake 'n scrape is an integral part of Bahamian culture and musical history, originating in the early century, when African slaves living in The Bahamas, sought to make music on whatever objects were available to them:

- carpenter's saw: scraped with piece of metal to form rhythm.
- skin of goat or sheep: stretched over pork barrels to create drums
- conch shell: blown to produce sound of a horn
- tin tubs with length of wood and fishing line: bass violins
- combs covered with paper: harmonica

Another instrument favoured by the rake 'n scrape band, was the gin bottle and nail. Since Key brand gin had raised letters on the side of the bottle, one could scrape the letters with a nail or utensil, to produce a sound that augmented the rhythm of the band. Accordions were also part of the rake 'n scrape ensemble, when available. Today, the rake 'n scrape tradition still thrives in the Bahamas. Traditional instruments are mixed with contemporary rhythms and songs to create a unique musical genre.

(I record Rupert Buckley's songs. His voice is on a reel, in the cassette machine fastened to the gallery wall. Now, anyone who wants to can press the **Play** button, to hear Rupert's raptures and laments.)

Eye of the Hurricane

I tell her I'm worried. "He'll be back," says the fisherman's wife, "Dutch Boy is a survivor. Finds fresh water beneath the ocean floor, never surfaces empty-handed. A diviner of the deep."

Only a few weeks remaining in Deadman's Cay.

The Fisherman's Wife picks up a stick from the sand, tracing a faint line around a fallen cluster of sea grapes, "Don't let his quiet way fool you. Passion swirls around Dutch Boy. He's like the hurricane's eye where there lies a great stillness, that strange unsettling peace in the middle of the storm until out of silence itself the wind resumes its howling."

Lobsters Don't Bark

Chile why do you walk a lobster on such blue blue ribbon? *Cause Ma'am, lobster don't bark and dey know all deep sea secrets . . .* the kid says to me, his countenance serious like a woodcut print. He strips a honeycomb clean with his teeth and picks up his crustacean, lodging it in the crook of his arm to join his friends who are perched high in the branches of a tamarind tree, ringing handbells and teetering like canaries.

☙

The Seafarer's Glowing Wake

"When we were first married, he'd take me fishing at night, to show me creatures called *sea candles.*" The fisherman's wife wades in, unties the boat and pushes us away from the dock. "I remember a v-shaped wake glowing an eerie, otherworldly green behind our boat. Sparks everywhere. I tried lowering my hand into the water to pull up a sample of the cascade, but my handful never contained the spectral stuff I was seeing." She takes a drag of her cigarette, exhales. "Tonight's too close to full moon, we won't see much," she says, glancing astern. "He showed me fish that had glowing eyes embedded in their skin, flashing about like fireworks underwater. Sometimes we'd dive in to swim with the glow." I spot a lanternfish that emits a blue-green luminescence, before quickly swimming away. The fisherman's wife flicks her cigarette into the water. The ember sizzles a moment and dies. "Ha! Je me souviens . . . our light shows, years ago. When we swam in permanent twilight . . ." and with that, she snaps out of her midnight reverie and steers the boat back toward the shoreline. In the moonlight, her hair roots are growing out a yellowish-grey. It's unlike her to forget to touch up. The top of her head has become a neglected halo of sugarcane.

☙

Hamilton's Cave

In Hamilton's Cave we're pitted, etched, dissolved. Stone faces tell us that everything rusts on this island: metals, the voice of the mockingbird, the pale line around the ring finger. There's only one exception to the rule: bats cluster deep in ridges and tunnels. Pyramids of guano outlive us and remain pure, silent and black as the unlit cave. No imperfect rose or unstable chair, no shadow of a lesser state dancing upon these walls.

☙

Crab 'n Dough

4 Large Black Crabs,

2 lbs flour
3 tsp baking powder
1/2 tbsp cooking oil
1/2 tsp salt
2 cloves garlic
2 cups water.

Break off biters and legs.
Wash and drain in seafan.

Prepare dough by mixing all ingredients together,
knead.
Place 4 Large Black Crabs in pot,
add garlic and water.

Flatten dough to fit over crabs.

Cover pot and boil 30 minutes.

〰

Shark Notes

Hummingbirds need nectar to survive.
Sharks must swim to breathe.
If they stop swimming they die.

No skeleton for my museum, sharks are boneless.
Only their teeth and vertebrae are calcified but even this
isn't true bone since it's dead when functional.

TIGER SHARK
Hyena of the sea. Predator scavenger. Serrated and hooked teeth that tear
open hard-shelled prey such as turtles, sea birds, rays, octopus, dolphins,
sea snakes. Tin cans, shoes, license plates. Hold a tiger (shark) by its tail,
turn it upside down it will relax in a pain free trance called *tonic
immobility.*

LEMON SHARK
Requiem shark with deep yellow back and teeth that catch slippery fish.
Residing near the surface of water and at moderate depths, frequenting
bays, docks, river mouths. Most active around twilight and dawn.

Great White Shark

Pretty killer. Dark eyes grinning. Clean, elegant lines, moves with a smooth, hypnotic grace that many of us envy.

Hammerhead Shark

Mouth behind eyes.

Light-sensitive. Superior sense of smell and hearing, listening for low frequency vibrations like those made by wounded fish.

Head swings from side to side like a metal detector, sampling water with the nose. Swimming in zigzag for miles to track the scent of wounded prey.

Nurse Shark

Disinterested interest. Slothful, grazing sea cow. The only shark that doesn't need to keep moving to breathe. Nicknamed Carpet Sharks, sinking to the ocean floor. Skin like sandpaper. Largesadeyes. One of the most docile animals of the sea.

∝

Casket of Pomegranates

"Is it still the same back home?" a faint voice inquires in the dark.
"Sometimes I wonder if—" the voice breaks off. A leathery hand lifts a
rotting fruit from the grass, aiming at the shadow of a bird. Her husband is
away at sea again. In my backyard we watch screech owls pluck doves
from thatch roofs one by one. In the last three weeks, her hair has grown
another inch of grey.

The fisherman's wife has dreams fermenting
in Aphrodite's casket
of pomegranates.

The fuchsia lipstick is gone.

❧

Display Panel: CHICKCHARNIES

This legendary creature resembles an elf and has piercing crimson eyes, three fingers, three toes and a tail by which it hangs from tall pine trees. It is believed that the chickcharnie forms its nest in the pine trees by joining two trees together at the top. If the beholder sneers at the little creature, his head will turn completely around permanently. If the beholder treats him with respect he will be blessed with good luck for the rest of his life.

Bonacorde

The fisherman's wife takes me to Bonacorde beach and tells me about the
worst hurricane in Bahamian history. "A rogue wave tossed one family
toward the heavens. They landed high in the hills, hanged by their hair
from silk cotton trees like ornaments. No time to tie up the mule, bake
johnnycake, or board the house. No time to detect a storm in the smell of
the sea, layering of clouds, absence of birds. All but a black rooster who
crowed three times before day broke." We've come to this beach because
a family of dolphins lives nearby. When there is a blue moon the dolphins
come out. We are quiet. The fisherman's wife slips her sandals off and
wades into the water, sarong and all. "I'll sing them a lullaby now watch
how they'll appear and dance then disappear." *Just like you*, I think I hear her
say but she's so far gone I can't be sure.

∞

Mailboat

The boat carrying letters and parcels destined for Deadman's Cay
never did arrive. No Gravol, no Muskol, no paper umbrellas for tropical
drinks. Phone echoes, voices from another life, still ring in my ears.

Where palm trees have grown legs, walking away from sunlight and birds
have passed but briefly, always migrating, always on their way Elsewhere,
I am here. At vespers on this rock I've prayed to a god whose eyes cut red
like a million tiny cave shrimp. Deluded and blue-blind, believing that the
sandfly bite which never healed has healed O spent sky of the tropics.

❧

Clouds Drift Past

Dutch Boy returns to Deadman's Cay the week I fly away. He tells the
fisherman's wife that he never reached Canada, but he'd seen more land
and water than he ever dreamt of. He tells her he feels tired, that he
doesn't think he's meant for travel after all.

He tells her to bid me farewell.

I see him once more when I walk along the highway, past the old sloop
sailboat marooned beneath the cork tree. His arms are folded in a diamond
behind his head and he stares at the clear blue sky. Clouds drift past now
and again, like faint fronds of plankton. *There can be nothing else,* he
reminds himself, as I raise my arm to greet him. I pause a moment,
wondering whether he'll rise to meet me. He turns briefly toward the
asphalt's middle distance, wavy in the rising heat. When he looks to the
spot I'm standing in and slowly, deliberately, shifts back toward the sky
again, I too, turn away. Lowering my arm and wiping my brow, I continue
down the road.

∾

By Your Still Pale Skin

We swim across Dean's Blue Hole, then build a fire on the beach. She lights the kindling, forms the teepee around it, laughing, "Good thing we're Canadian you'll never find a Bahamian who can make a campfire." I ask, "Don't you miss the seasons?" She replies, "I was never one for seasons," then, "I knew you would leave. By your still pale skin and those blue veins across your temples like blades of grass in a delftware scene, I knew home was calling you."

This, my last night, my last dawn, in Deadman's Cay.

Tongue of the Ocean

Everyone asks, *what happened to the fisherman's wife, what about Dutch Boy?* I could invent. But after leaving Deadman's Cay, I can't know what happens.

Of two things I am certain:

#1   Dutch Boy won't leave his island again until a barge carries him away. I don't blame him, it is his Paradise.

#2   Since Love found the fisherman's wife she will also remain here. She won't return to Our Cold Continent and if, one day, her beloved stays out to sea too long, the fisherman's wife will walk into the tongue of the ocean in search of him. Without looking back toward Deadman's Cay.

So you will never meet either of them (I am not addressing my ex-lover this time).

☞

Especially After a Snowfall

Did I return to the old Alsatian or did Dutch Boy capture my heart? The day of my departure I found the nest of a hummingbird at my doorstep. When I picked it up a pink conch pearl fell onto the ground and I'm not reaching for effect when I say it was shaped like a tear. It's a pendant now. An invisible mesh of kelp will sometimes snag my tendons for no apparent reason, after a snowfall when our landscape has a blue hue to it and all is calm. On these occasions, especially, I'm thinking of Dutch Boy.

✺

Letters from Deadman's Cay

i

I hear whistling and the voices of small children where there are no children to be found. I recall Obeah tales and imagine a sea wolf with sea glass eyes leading all the children into the island's ocean hole. Would I see the children's dark heads bobbing up and down, slick and surfacing on nights without moonlight?

I wanted badly to compose a message for a bottle that I would toss into the blue hole before I left the island. The fisherman's wife tells me that whatever falls into a blue hole eventually washes up somewhere along the seashore. The island's goats and sheep jump like lemmings into these holes, one and one and one, carcasses white with tide, washed up and tangled in nets among silver minnows, set gleaming on their eyes to pay the ferryman. But I never composed a message.

I threw the bottle into the blue hole
capped and sealed, containing nothing.

There was a yucca plant I passed each day on my way to the museum, where local people carved names and messages onto hard, green leaves. I thought to myself, *I'll* carve a single word for the yucca before I'm gone, one word to outlive me.

I never came up with that word, that precise meaning.
I left my green space blank.

ii

The invisible, mute sandflies never ceased to inflict their idiot hurt onto my flesh, they plucked and sucked words from me and each tiny white bump is one word less I have to say, each scar is a braille mark I can't explain in speech. Small scars remain where once there were words, where long ago, I thought I had something to say about love.

iii

Looking back on my island, my rock, my pumiced heart, what flashes
before my mind is a single image of a pink plastic pig I found washed
upon the shore on an empty beach near Chimney Rock, where waves
laughed and whispered, *"mortal, weary mortal, we're immortal. . . ."* When
I plucked the pig from the surge, pristine and shining and newborn, I
wailed and clutched the toy in my hands. I sat with him the length of the
day and as the sun set, I propped him high on a rock, safely wedged in the
cliff and staring out to sea. He would be my new companion on the island.
When I returned the next evening, he was gone.

iv

I've left no marks on this island. In my suitcase, I bring home a black buoy encrusted with coral, a conch shell to hear the ocean. I carry the skeleton of a crab so light I can't feel the thing even as I hold it in the palm of my hand, and a jar of sea glass, smooth and rounded, each shard collected for every day I spent here. Will I ever be gone from Deadman's Cay? I leave a piece of me on the cliffs of Chimney Rock and I know that when the reaper comes and the rewind of images curl around my soul, I'll see turquoise and sand and sunsets flashing green, black roosters gliding toward palm trees

silent at last.

≪

Leaving

To drink immortality from the 7-Up cup the stewardess brings on a tray.
The okra pod bleeds a yawning film in my mouth, fine quill powder from
the archaic porcupine fish blows sleep on my face,   slowing

                                             down

my

                pulse.

                      Snowbirdsnowbirdsnowbirdsnowbird.

This is the place for the Almost Dead. When we die, another generation
grows on our dorsal fin.

Renewed, like the sky after a hurricane.

☞

NINA BERKHOUT was born and raised in Calgary, Alberta. After completing a degree in Classical Studies at the University of Calgary, she went on to the University of Toronto where she earned a MA in Museum Studies.

Letters from Deadman's Cay is based on Berkhout's experience living on a remote out-island in The Bahamas, where she worked to set up a community museum, collecting artifacts and recording the story of the island and its inhabitants.

Berkhout's poetry has been published in *Forum, Jones Av, Free Fall, Lichen, Grain, SEEDS,* and *Prairie Fire.* Her poetry was also shortlisted in *THIS* Magazine's 2001 Great Canadian Literary Hunt.